SHIRE NATURAL HISTORY

HARRIERS
of the British Isles

ROGER CLARKE

CONTENTS

Cover: *Male hen harrier landing at his nest with skylark prey.*

Series editor: Jim Flegg.

Copyright © 1990 by Roger Clarke. First published 1990.
Number 57 in the Shire Natural History series. ISBN 0 7478 0092 8.

British Library Cataloguing in Publication Data:
Clarke, Roger.
Harriers of the British Isles.
1. Great Britain. Harriers.
I. Title.
598.916

Printed in Great Britain by J. Thomas & Sons (Haverfordwest) Ltd,
st, Dyfed SA61 1XF.

Introduction

Harriers, the *Circus* genus, are open-country diurnal raptors (daytime-active birds of prey). Of slim build, with a longish tail and very long wings relative to body weight, their buoyancy in the air allows them to forage for extended periods. Alternately flapping and gliding on wings held up in a shallow dihedral (V shape), they fly as low to the ground as necessary to maximise their chances of surprising small bird, mammal and reptile prey. Rank vegetation and the lie of the land are used to hide their approach. They both look and listen for prey, their pronounced facial discs concealing large ears which they probably use in a similar manner to the unrelated owls; when they balance a sound between their ears, such as a rustling in the grass, the head is positioned so as to be looking straight at the correct place without having to have seen the animal responsible. Prey are mostly pinned to the ground with the aid of exceptionally long legs.

SPECIES

The number of species of harrier worldwide is thought to be ten, comprising: the spotted harrier (*Circus assimilis*) of Australia; the long-winged harrier (*C. buffoni*) and the cinereous harrier (*C. cinereus*), both of South America; the marsh harrier (*C. aeruginosus*) of Europe, Africa, Asia and Australasia; the African marsh harrier (*C. ranivorus*) of southern Africa; the black harrier (*C. maurus*) of South Africa; the pied harrier (*C. melanoleucus*) of eastern Asia; the hen harrier (*C. cyaneus*) of Europe, Asia and North America; the pallid harrier (*C. macrourus*) of eastern Europe, Asia and Africa; and Montagu's harrier (*C. pygargus*) of Europe, Asia and Africa. Most species are migratory, the northern hemisphere species occupying the southern parts of their ranges in winter. The exact number of species is the subject of debate, mainly because the forms of the marsh harrier occurring in some regions are treated as separate species by some ornithologists, and because it is sometimes argued that the cinereous harrier is just a race of the hen harrier. However, if only the African marsh harrier is taken as a species separate from other marsh harriers (beause of its significantly smaller size and distinct plumage), and the northern harrier, formerly called 'marsh hawk', (*C. cyaneus hudsonius*) of North America is taken to be a race of the hen harrier, but the cinereous harrier is not, then ten is the correct number. Harriers cover all the world's open land except the Arctic, Antarctica and most deserts.

Four of the ten species occur in the British Isles. A mainly summer resident (April to mid September), the marsh harrier has bred in increasing numbers in England, mainly along the East Anglian coast, but its range is extending quite rapidly. The hen harrier's breeding population is badly persecuted by game interests and is confined largely to Scotland and Ireland, although small numbers have bred under protection in northern England and Wales. Out of the breeding season, it is a fairly widespread but scarce species. Significant numbers of hen harriers wintering in eastern and southern England (about mid October to mid April) are probably mainly continental immigrants. More and more winter communal roost sites have been found since the late 1970s. Montagu's harrier is a rare summer visitor, breeding in tiny numbers mainly in eastern and southern England. The pallid harrier is an extremely rare vagrant in western Europe, with just three recorded in Britain.

FIELD IDENTIFICATION

Harriers are somewhat variable in colouration. In the males this is often a guide to their age, with fully adult ones being more typical or 'text-book' specimens. Of the females, the marsh harrier is the most variable. Because the marsh harrier is the largest species and the female is larger than the male, she is the biggest harrier of all. Larger than a crow, her fairly uniform brown colour often makes her look a dark bird, but she usually has a yellowish cream crown and chin, and similarly coloured leading edges to the wings up to where they angle back at the carpal (wrist) joints. Some females have further yellow-cream splashes on the breast and elsewhere. Juvenile marsh harriers are difficult to distinguish from the female, although they tend to be a more uniform, darker chocolate brown and have a ginger to cream coloured crown and chin, with little relief elsewhere. The underwing of an adult female shows contrast between the dark secondaries and the quite sandy primaries with dark tips, whereas the juvenile's underwing is uniformly dark apart from whitish bases to the primaries. The slimmer male acquires adult plumage in his second calendar year — a brown body dark above but rufous and streaked below, buff head, lavender-grey tail and wing panel, and black wing tips. A fine old male has a strikingly tricoloured appearance.

The hen harrier and the slimmer Montagu's harrier are very similar to each other. They are so similar that early ornithologists were unsure that they were separate species until the Devon naturalist Colonel George Montagu described the smaller species in the *Linnaean Transactions* in 1803. He called it the 'ash-coloured falcon'. Although adult males of both species are grey birds with black wing tips, they are told apart relatively easily; the Montagu's has generally darker, 'dirtier' grey upperparts, head and breast, black bars on the middle of the wings (one visible above, but two below) and rust-coloured streaks on white underparts, whereas the plainer male hen harrier has generally cleaner blue-grey upperparts, head and breast, and otherwise plain white underparts except for the black primaries and a dark trailing edge to the wing, which fades on the top with age but remains blackish on the underwing. Relatively young adult males have a brown cast to the back, becoming pure blue-grey with age. Apart from having a looser wing action and longer wings, the adult male pallid harrier differs from the hen harrier in having a white breast and a narrower wedge of black in the primaries.

The adult females are much more difficult to tell apart, both from each other and from hen harriers of either sex less than a year old. Further confusion is possible with the female pallid harrier. The dark brown upperparts, streaked underparts, white rumps and banded tails of all these birds are very similar, and the general term for such a bird is 'ringtail'. Any ringtail in the British Isles from October to mid April, however, is almost certainly a hen harrier. Otherwise, the best features distinguishing the rarer Montagu's harrier at other times of the year (although requiring some familiarity with hen harriers) are longer-looking slimmer wings, with three primaries prominently protruding at the wing tips rather than the four of the hen harrier, and a more willowy wing action. The face pattern of the Montagu's is more distinctive, with a dark cheek patch and noticeably whitish streaks above and below the eye. The female pallid harrier is similar to the Montagu's, except that the ruff forms a bold whitish collar behind the dark cheek patch and the dark bands on the underneath of the secondaries converge towards the body (beware a similar trait in the hen harrier). Juvenile hen harriers are virtually identical to the adult female, apart from the male's smaller size. The juvenile Montagu's and pallid harriers are plain rufous below, instead of brown-streaked like the great majority of juvenile hen harriers.

As with most birds of prey, the legs and cere are generally bright yellow (but the cere is greenish lemon in the marsh harrier). Although rarely useful to the observer in the field, the eye colour of harriers varies interestingly with age and sex. This has been most studied in the hen harrier. Male young soon show grey-brown irides, which turn yellow early in life. Females start life with chocolate-brown irides and can be sexed by this in the nest. But the background colour is yellow, which is gradually revealed over about five years. During this time the eyes gradually have less and less of what becomes a brown flecking. This feature is most useful for assessing age in close observation from a hide, and it is interesting to see the variation in published photographs of females at the nest. The eyes of a female of intermediate age look orange. The eye colours of Montagu's harrier follow very much the same pattern. Marsh harrier young of both sexes have brown irides, with similar changes occurring with age as in the other species.

Harriers are not very vocal birds. On breeding grounds various calls are made by the adults in courtship and when the male returns to the nest with food (described in the chapter on 'Breeding'), but at other times they are very much the silent hunters. Even at hen harrier communal winter roosts, readily audible calling is only very occasional and generally associated with alarm. However, vocal communication not normally audible to observers is quite frequent there (described under 'Communal roosting').

BASIC ECOLOGY

With one exception, all species of harrier nest on the ground, amongst rank vegetation. The spotted harrier is the only species to breed in trees, but its flat, rather unstable nest seems to indicate that it has moved up into trees relatively recently, perhaps as an evolutionary response to high predation pressure on the ground in the arid areas of Australia where it lives.

The more northerly breeding species are highly migratory, with only the hen harrier remaining in any numbers at temperate latitudes in the northern hemisphere. Outside the breeding season, communal roosting in rank vegetation on the ground has been noted in all species except the African marsh harrier, which is mate-specific and keeps a loose territory the year round, and the spotted harrier, which has yet to be studied in winter. Communal roosts attract hundreds of harriers in some parts of the world, but the habit is still widespread where numbers are relatively small. In Britain hen harrier roosts normally hold just a few birds each, and even single birds persist in using the same traditional sites.

Dimorphism

All harriers show reversed sexual size dimorphism (the females are larger than the males). Theories about the reasons for such dimorphism, found in many raptors, revolve around a more formidable female being more capable in defence of the nest and the ability of sexes of different sizes to tackle prey of different sizes, enabling a species to use a wider range of prey, and therefore obtain a greater quantity. In addition to this intraspecific (within a species) advantage, there is a similar interspecific (between species) advantage because of the further variation in weight and ratio of wing length to body weight between species. Table 1 shows weights and wing lengths of the species of harrier breeding in Britain and western Europe. The decrease in weight and increase in length of wing relative to body weight is gradual through these three 'sympatric' (living in the same region) species. Some similarity can be seen between the data for the male marsh harrier and the female hen harrier, also between the male hen harrier and the female Montagu's harrier, but staggered breeding seasons for these species ensures that males of the larger species are not still hunting fully in earnest by the time females of the smaller species are released from incubation and brooding of young chicks to hunt. This ensures that harriers of similar size are not competing for the same size-class of prey at the vital time when their young are so dependent on a continuous supply of food.

With the longest wings relative to body weight, the male Montagu's harrier can stay in the air longer, range further from the nest and live on smaller prey. At the other end of the scale, the large and not so agile female marsh harrier tends to hunt over long vegetation where the most can be made of surprising and trapping prey which she generally could not hope to catch in the open.

The plumage of the sexes is very dissimilar in adults of all species except the black harrier, the spotted harrier and the African marsh harrier. In the European species, adult males are grey above (although the marsh harrier is only partly so) and lighter below, but females are brown. The extent of the dissimilarities in plumage and size confused early ornithologists, who began to regard the 'ringtail' as a separate species to the grey 'hen-harrier'. It was again the late eighteenth-century and early nineteenth-century naturalist Colonel George Montagu who

4

1. *Ringtail hen harrier in characteristic flight.*
2. *Female marsh harrier.*

	Female	Female	Female	Male	Male	Male
	A Wing length (mm)	B Weight (grams)	Ratio A/B	A Wing length (mm)	B Weight (grams)	Ratio A/B
Species						
Marsh harrier	413	669	0.62	393	500	0.79
Hen harrier	376	527	0.71	338	346	0.98
Montagu's harrier	372	370	1.01	365	261	1.40

Table 1. *Mean weights and wing lengths of the three species of harrier breeding in the British Isles. The wing length is measured from the carpal (wrist) joint to the tip of the longest primary feather. Source of data: Cramp and Simmons, 1977.*

helped to resolve the matter. He took a brood of three young into captivity, forcing an early change in plumage by plucking 'quill and tail' feathers and was 'highly gratified' to find grey feathers growing through on the smallest bird, the one he suspected to be a male.

The difference in plumage probably evolved to make the female inconspicuous on the nest and the male less conspicuous as he flies above prey. Most species have a white rump patch, which may have some visual function. It certainly helps human observers to see ringtails when they otherwise blend with their background.

Distribution, migration and mortality

BREEDING RANGES AND POPULATION TRENDS

The hen harrier traditionally nests on moorland, most sites being at altitudes of 200-50 metres (650-820 feet) above sea level. In recent decades many of these upland areas have been rapidly covered by blanket forestry. Harriers will remain to breed in the resulting young conifer plantations, but only if there is still open moorland close by where they can hunt in the way for which they are adapted. A temporary increase in the field vole (*Microtus agrestis*) population and the absence of human persecution of birds of prey in plantations have greatly encouraged the species and have had a dramatic effect on its distribution. In some areas of Scotland planting has occurred piecemeal and has provided a useful patchwork of habitats for the hen harrier to increase its population and extend its breeding range. But in Ireland, for example, an increase in numbers has soon turned into fast decline as large plantations have grown into mature trees *en bloc*. Odd pairs will persist in nesting at favoured sites for perhaps twenty years while the trees grow around them. But eventually the trees will close over smaller gaps and make access impossible for the ground-nesting harrier, or they will severely curtail its hunting range, even if it nests outside the plantation. Few nests have been found in areas later felled of trees and replanted, boding very ill for the future of the species in forestry areas.

Illegal destruction of nests by shooting interests is a constantly limiting factor on prime harrier-nesting territory on grouse moors, and a fresh outlook is needed on the part of landowners and gamekeepers if the hen harrier is not to become dangerously rare. There is a great deal of potential public interest in such a beautiful bird of prey, which should be mobilised to the benefit of the species. Much heather moorland has now been planted with conifers, and this may continue where there is even just a temporary cyclic decline in grouse stocks. The result is that the pressure on remaining grouse moors is intense, and with traditional attitudes prevailing the hen harrier stands little chance. A peak of perhaps seven

6

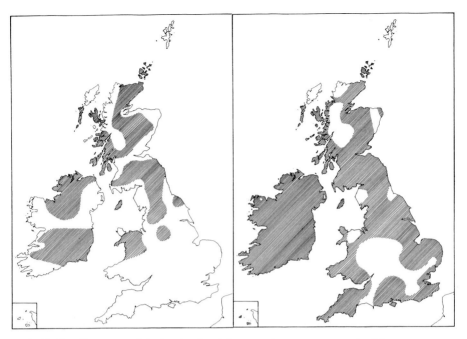

3 (left). *Breeding range of the hen harrier. It is extremely scarce over much of the range.*
4 (right). *Wintering range of the hen harrier.*

hundred nests in Britain and Ireland in the 1970s had undoubtedly dwindled considerably by the late 1980s.

Shooting interests have shaped the population trends of all birds of prey, especially in the nineteenth century, when the hen harrier was exterminated from all but a few remote parts of the British Isles. Its ground nesting and the typical boldness of adults in defence of their young made the species an easy target. A few survived in Orkney, the Outer Hebrides and Ireland, where there are few grouse moors. However, as a rare species, they were then very actively sought by collectors, for both their skins and their eggs. At the beginning of the First World War the species was perhaps at its lowest level, after which it greatly benefited from a depression in active gamekeepering during both world wars and it began to recolonise mainland Scotland, assisted to some extent by new attitudes and bird protection laws. The species was therefore in a position to take quick advantage of the widespread for-estry planting since the Second World War. There is no evidence that hen harriers in Britain were significantly affected by the organochlorine pesticides which entered the food chain and in other raptors caused abnormal behaviour and frustration of breeding due to eggshell thinning in the 1960s and 1970s, as well as direct mortality. Breeding away from predominantly arable areas, the hen harrier increased at a time when other harriers, peregrines and sparrowhawks more exposed to pesticide residues in prey were experiencing a population decline.

The comeback of the marsh harrier to eastern England is a prime example of what public interest can achieve. It became extinct in Britain by 1900 because of habitat loss and human persecution, but active conservation of a few birds recolonising two parts of the Norfolk Broads from 1911 eventually led to a gradual extension of nesting to other sites as more reed-bed nature reserves were established and gamekeepers became less numerous because of the Second World War and social change. However, the species almost became extinct in Britain again in the 1960s, probably because of direct mortality due to dangerous agricultural pesticides rather than eggshell thinning, which was about 10 per cent for this species. A steady revival began in the 1970s with some control of pesticides, the establishment of more marshland bird reserves in East Anglia and active protection of the species by the RSPB and others, aided by public money and participation. A large population of marsh harriers nearby in the Netherlands is likely to have provided immigrants — the large areas of reed-bed in the Polders were fast being reclaimed for farming at the time. Most nests are likely to occur in Norfolk and Suffolk for some time to come, but the species is breeding increasingly in surrounding counties and beyond. The breeding distribution has a strong bias towards the coast. Figures published by the Rare Breeding Birds Panel record eleven nests in 1976 and 33 in 1986.

The status of Montagu's harrier in Britain is precarious in the extreme. No historical evidence exists to show that there ever was a large population in the British Isles, but perhaps seventy to eighty pairs bred in the mid 1950s. A rapid decrease after that culminated in years during the mid 1970s when no successful nests were reported. Although no analysis was published for this species that directly implicated pesticides, the timing of this decline to the verge of extinction in Britain coincided exactly with the rapid declines in populations of other raptors due to dangerous chemicals. During the following ten years anything between one and seven pairs were recorded breeding, with just a suggestion of a sustained increase towards the end of that period. Although this species has often nested on heathland and marshland in the past, almost all pairs in England now nest in cereal fields in eastern and southern coastal counties, so that breeding birds have to be found and the co-operation of farmers sought to avoid unintentional destruction of nests by routine farming operations.

There are instances of breeding by Montagu's harriers on record for Scotland — in three years in the 1950s for Perthshire and in 1953 for Kirkcudbrightshire. A small colony persisted in Anglesey in Wales, beginning with a single pair in 1945, but, after years with up to five

5. The spotted harrier at its nest. This Australian species is the only harrier to nest in trees.

6 (left). *Male hen harrier showing the 'dingy' back of a relatively young male. The plumage turns more pure blue-grey with age.*

7 (right). *Male Montagu's harrier*

pairs breeding, it ceased after 1964 — at about the same time as the crash in the population elsewhere in Britain. The species is a rare breeder in Ireland, but little information is available.

MIGRATION AND DISTRIBUTION OUT OF THE BREEDING SEASON

Montagu's harrier is the only wholly migrant harrier breeding in the British Isles. Arriving from late April, it leaves in August or September for a wintering range in Africa south of the Sahara Desert. Because harriers are so buoyant in the air, they do not need to seek short sea crossings or rely on thermals for lift like many other migrants. Montagu's harriers therefore migrate on a broad front across the Mediterranean. The few ringing recoveries of first-summer Montagu's in Europe indicate that many may stay in Africa as non-breeders until their second summer.

Nearly all British marsh harriers migrate. Leaving mainly in September, some are known to go to Africa, where birds ringed at nests in England have been recovered in Senegal and Mauritania. Others may linger in France, Spain and around the Mediterranean, mixing with birds that could be resident there the year through. Those that do winter in Britain have been recorded mainly on the East Anglian and South Wales coasts. The return passage reaches the British Isles mainly in April.

The movements of hen harriers are highly complicated. A very few winter in North Africa, but the general pattern is a switch from pockets of breeding area, limited in size by nesting habitat, to much more widespread occurrence at moderate and southern latitudes in western Europe. Birds from northerly breeding areas may generally winter further south than those breeding at intermediate latitudes such as Scotland. Deserting Norway, northern Sweden and Finland in autumn, hen harriers tend to retreat from southern Sweden and Denmark too in

9

mid-winter months. Also, because of a later start to their breeding, those from more northerly breeding populations may leave wintering areas later than Scottish birds. Certainly, some adult hen harriers are still using communal roost sites in eastern England in April, when Scottish birds are already displaying on breeding grounds. A proportion of birds from intermediate latitudes are resident in breeding areas the year through, whilst others from the same places migrate.

Hen harriers frequent open country of many types in winter, but especially heathland, downland, river valleys, coastal marshes and low-lying flat plains such as the Fens of Lincolnshire, Cambridgeshire and Norfolk. Eastern and southern England, from about the Humber estuary round to Cornwall, hold a winter population of a few hundred. The coastal regions of Wales attract a few, south-west Scotland quite a large concentration, and Orkney, the most northerly wintering place for the species in Europe, retains a significant number from its breeding population. Elsewhere in the British Isles, rather few small pockets of winter distribution have been found. Records are especially scarce in the English Midlands.

Hen harriers remaining in Orkney during the winter tend to be females, which are able to outlast severe weather better than the smaller males and are less agile than the males at catching passerine prey, which is more readily available elsewhere at this time. Females rely more on voles and are also more capable of killing larger resident prey such as lagomorphs (rabbits and hares). Counts at communal winter roosts have found a significantly higher proportion of grey males in the west of Britain until March. This may be due to a tendency of males to follow migrating passerines to the south-west.

Hen harriers wintering in eastern and southern England show very mixed origins, with recoveries of birds from the Netherlands, Scotland and Wales, also single birds from Sweden and Finland, where only small proportions of the breeding populations have been ringed. Recoveries of birds ringed in Scotland occur mainly in Scotland, but a few have been widespread over Europe.

Very few hen harrier communal winter roost sites were known in the British Isles before the mid 1970s, but around two hundred have been found since. About half of the sites were used every winter from their discovery to 1985/6, with about half of those being in eastern and southern England. A much lower proportion of sites in other regions of England are regularly used. It seems probable that there was either a boost in the European population of the species or a westerly shift in its winter distribution in the late 1970s; the same upsurge in roost records has been reported from other west European countries, such as the Netherlands, Belgium and France. Prolonged snow and easterly winds in early 1979 brought an extraordinary influx of hen harriers to the east and south coasts of England, resulting in a sharp increase in the rate of discovery of hen harrier roosts that winter. Reports from northern France and Belgium indicate a general influx in western Europe that winter. Many of these birds may have come from Scandinavian breeding populations but there is no corroborative evidence, apart from a peak in the autumn migration figures at Falsterbo in Sweden at that time, but based on only 221 birds because of the dispersed broad-front migration characteristic of the genus.

MORTALITY

Ringing recoveries show that mortality is heaviest amongst harriers less than one year old; more than 60 per cent of hen harriers ringed in the nest and recovered are dead within twelve months. Birds recovered beyond that time seem to attain an average age of a little over 3½ years, but a few do have quite long lives; the record is sixteen years. However, recoveries reported are likely to have a heavy bias away from birds shot, and shooting may impose a different pattern of unrecorded mortality. Apart from the uninformative 'found dead' category, the more common reported causes of death are collision with road vehicles, striking overhead wires and entanglement with barbed wire.

The migratory marsh and Montagu's harriers run the gauntlet of an almost uncontrollable mania in southern Europe for shooting any type of bird, and many harriers bred in the British Isles are killed in this way. The statistics are very frightening indeed; the ratios of birdwatchers to 'hunters' in France, Spain and Italy have been reckoned to be 1:1050, 1:500 and 1:22,300 respectively. The task of educating the populace is being undertaken, but there is an enormous inertia to be overcome. Organisations such as the ICBP and RSPB that actively pursue this work deserve the fullest support. Also vital is the project by the International Union for the Conservation of Nature to conserve the floodplain of the river Niger delta in west Africa beyond the Sahara — the Sahel. There the whole fragile ecosystem that supports so many migrants from Britain, including significant numbers of marsh and Montagu's harriers, is under threat from drought caused by climatic change and barrage schemes upstream.

Feeding

STRUCTURAL ADAPTATIONS

Long wings and light wing-loadings enable harriers to be on the wing for perhaps half the day and put in the amount of 'cold' searching their method of hunting requires to find enough food. This is in contrast to the short bursts of active hunting practised by many other raptors. Harriers have somewhat forward-facing, concave facial discs, which help direct both eyes forward to focus together in binocular vision and gauge distance and speed to a fine degree. Their ears are much larger than those of other diurnal raptors of similar size. These are set back in the concave facial discs, which assist with trapping sounds. The ear opening and an area of bare skin extending down from the opening towards the bill are covered by soft long feathers growing from behind the eye. In a crescent behind the facial disc a dense ruff of short stiff curved-back feathers helps to direct sounds into the ear. These features are similar to those found in owls — an example of convergent evolution — although solely for searching dense vegetation in the case of harriers, which are not active in the dark.

To assist with speed in striking and reaching down into vegetation, harriers have evolved long legs. As in all raptors, their sharply taloned toes automatically extend when the leg is outstretched towards prey and contract as the harrier's weight comes down and pulls on tendons in the legs.

HUNTING

All species of harrier have the same basic method of hunting. Flying rather

8. *Male hen harrier: the long ear coverts held back to reveal the large ear opening and a patch of bare skin characteristic in harriers.*

9. *Male marsh harrier and his young.*

10 (left). *The black harrier in South Africa.*

11 (right). *Male pallid harrier.*

12 (left). *Female hen harrier landing at her nest.*

13 (right). *Ringtail hen harrier. The darker secondaries denote an immature.*

14. *Melanistic morph male Montagu's harrier and his young. There are a few records of melanistic individuals of this species occurring in Britain.*

slowly, usually low over the ground, they flap for a few metres and then gracefully glide on for a similar distance. They often fly into the wind to slow down ground speed — particularly useful when looking down into tall vegetation for prey. Rank vegetation and features such as ditches conceal small bird, mammal and reptile quarry but also mask the harrier's approach. When it happens upon its quarry, the harrier can strike with speed, within a small gap in vegetation or just beyond a low obstacle. Where it cannot strike immediately, the harrier hesitates over its quarry until it finds the right moment or has to fly on. It dives straight down on prey, feet first and wings up-raised, or stalls by spreading its tail and slices down through the air in a character-istic sideways pirouette. If the quarry is not noticed until passed over, the harrier can double back with amazing speed, assisted by the wind it has been flying into.

The larger and less manoeuvrable har-riers tend to hunt over taller vegetation, where it is easier to approach prey and more difficult for it to escape quickly. This is why the marsh harrier generally hunts from a greater height than the other British species, so as to be able to look down into tall cover such as reeds, and then dropping down suddenly when it detects something of interest. In a strong wind a marsh harrier may simply hang into it over a likely place, maintain-ing position with occasional wing flaps.

By no means all strikes are successful. A study of wintering northern harriers in North America, for example, found that 15.1 per cent of strikes were successful on salt-marsh and 5.8 per cent on wet meadows and pasture.

Extensive searching, or 'quartering', for prey requires wide open spaces, especially because so much hunting is done on a linear basis, following ditches and habitat edges. It has been estimated that the hen harrier, for example, 'perhaps flies about 100 miles (160 km) every day of its life'. Harriers will some-times flush whole flocks of birds up to waterfowl size, lazily flying towards them with no apparent hope of catching any-thing, but in the process checking them out for any sick or injured individuals

which might be easy prey. Another mode of hunting is fast, low and directed at catching birds. The male hen harrier is best at this, because it has the right combination of wing length and body weight to make it the most manoeuvrable harrier at speed. Harriers can also occa-sionally be seen foraging through tree tops, obviously seeking to catch pas-serines. Hunting for small mammals requires less agility and occasionally har-riers 'still hunt', standing on the ground and looking around for prey such as voles.

On rare occasions a harrier can be seen diving at quite large quarry, such as an adult pheasant (*Phasianus colchicus*). These attacks are usually easily resisted by the quarry and are rarely successful, although the remains of pheasant, for example, are sometimes found in harrier pellets which contain lead shot too, indicating that a wounded bird has been killed or the harrier has fed on carrion. Harriers do hunt smaller and young gamebirds, but these form just a propor-tion of their diet.

DIET

Hen harrier prey has been the subject of a number of studies in different parts of Britain (tables 2 and 3). Depending on the researcher's methods, the data are based on observation of prey brought to the nest or on pellet analysis. Experience of pellet analysis has traditionally been gained with owl pellets, based on the bone remains in which they are rich. Harrier pellets (and pellets of other diurnal raptors) contain far fewer bone remains because their digestion is stronger and they often strip off flesh instead of swallowing prey whole. Identi-fication of prey from pellets is therefore difficult and often has to be based on fur and feathers alone. The proportions of the diet made up of mammals or birds tend to vary greatly, depending on the abundance and vulnerability of each. The principal mammals taken in Britain are voles and rabbit (*Oryctolagus cuniculus*). In Ireland, however, where the popula-tion of hen harriers flourished in the 1960s and early 1970s, there are almost no voles. The range of birds taken can be very wide. For example, more than thirty species have been identified by the author in pellets from New Forest roost sites — anything that can be surprised at ground level, and occasionally on the tree tops. But small open-country passerines tend to dominate, such as skylark (*Alauda arvensis*) and meadow pipit (*Anthus pratensis*). Harriers do sometimes take gamebird chicks, but not to the exclusion of everything else. Debate rages, especially as to the taking of red grouse (*Lagopus lagopus*) by hen harriers and the effect it has on the grouse-shooter's bag. Studies of this have been undertaken, but their conclusions about the proportion of grouse taken vary widely and there is still a lot to learn about the relationship between hen harriers and red grouse. Many hen harrier nests are destroyed annually and the adult birds shot by game interests, quite illegally. The hen harrier, together with all other raptors, is fully protected under British law.

Marsh and Montagu's harrier prey are less extensively studied in Britain. Breeding season studies of marsh harrier prey have been published from Titchwell Marsh RSPB reserve and another coastal part of East Anglia. The principal prey at Titchwell were juvenile starlings (*Sturnus vulgaris*), pheasants (mainly wild poults) and young rabbits. These three together made up about half of the prey in the

	Orkney	Kincardineshire	Galloway
Number of prey items	482	758	209
Percentage:			
Birds			
meadow pipit	10	45	22
other passerines	22	5	30
waders	9	2	4
grouse	7	34	27
other	0	0	3
Mammals			
rabbit/hare	47	11	0
voles	4	2	4
other	1	1	1
Invertebrates			
beetles	0	0	9

Table 2. *Hen harrier prey identified at British nest sites. Sources: Picozzi, 1980; Picozzi, 1978; Watson, 1977.*

	Orkney (farmland grazing)	Dumfries and Galloway (coastal)	Strathclyde (upland)	Cambridgeshire (fenland)
Number of prey items	489	160	26	400
Percentage:				
Birds				
starling	19	1	4	0
skylark	} 13	2	0	24
other passerines		77	8	44
gamebirds	0	0	23	2
waders	0	2	0	2
Mammals				
rabbit/hare	16	0	54	15
small rodents and insectivores (mainly voles)	52	18	11	13

Table 3. *Hen harrier prey identified from pellets collected at British winter communal roost sites. Sources: Picozzi and Cuthbert, 1982; Marquiss, 1980; Clarke, 1988.*

15. *Hen harrier pellets.*

other study, but a wide range of other birds and mammals was recorded too. No comprehensive study of the food of Montagu's harrier in Britain has yet been published. Fragments of information from various sources suggest that it is comprised of open-country passerines, small mammals, lizards and young rabbits or brown hares (*Lepus europaeus*).

It is often unclear whether invertebrate remains found in pellets were taken

16. *Female Montagu's harrier with nesting material, which is carried either in the bill or in the feet.*

directly by the harrier or were the food of their prey. Invertebrates are likely to be most important in the diet of the smaller Montagu's harrier. Other foods known to be eaten at times by harriers are eggs and stranded fish.

Breeding

Harriers take two or three years to come to full maturity, but a number of instances are known where birds have bred in their second calendar year. This is more noticeable for males, which are still in brown plumage at the time. Male hen harriers in ringtail plumage and male marsh harriers with no grey in their plumage breed successfully quite often, but male Montagu's of similar age may not. The position is not so clear for females, which are less easily aged, but the information available suggests that they are more likely to breed in their second calendar year than males.

Harriers hide their nests on the ground, amongst rank vegetation of various kinds. The eggs of all species are white, and incubation and brooding are generally done entirely by the female. During incubation, the exact position of the nest is given away only by perhaps two or three visits each day by the male bringing food. Calling to the female that it is safe to leave the nest, he may fly to a platform or 'cock's nest' he has built nearby, the female going over to him to take the food there. Often, however, the food is transferred from male to female in the air — a particularly beautiful piece of harrier behaviour called 'the pass'. Flying over with legs down, clearly showing prey held in his talons, the male is met in the air by the female flying up beneath him and with lightning speed she reaches out with her feet to catch the prey as he drops it, or to take it direct from him. The female does this in a sideways banking movement or sometimes flips over on her back. The female hunts too when the young no longer need constant brooding. The young become quite active in the immediate vicinity of the nest, which can be trampled out of all recognition, and

17. *Male marsh harrier carrying nesting material.*

when they fledge they soon take passes of food from the adults and may remain with at least one of their parents for a few weeks until they disperse.

SEMI-COLONIAL NESTING AND POLYGYNY

In some situations harriers tend to nest in loose colonies, and this may be important to the survival of individual nests, although any mechanism at work is not fully understood and isolated pairs often seem to breed perfectly well. Linked to

this is the sporadic occurrence of polygyny (more than one female mated to a male) in all British species. In Orkney, where the population of hen harriers has been studied over many years, polygyny began to be recorded frequently as numbers of breeding birds reached a high level. Subsequently the numbers of females continued to increase whilst the numbers of males remained relatively stable. Although one-year-old males were mostly monogamous, older males often supported three or even four

18. *Hen harrier eggs in nest.*

nests. Nests in such harems were grouped together, although the distance from nest to nest was often a kilometre or more. The dynamics of the Orkney population suggested that a point was reached where the breeding habitat could support no further males. But where a male was experienced and capable, there were benefits in having a harem, even though he could supply less food to each of several nests than he could to one and, on average, more young were reared in a monogamous nest. It may be important that the best males can each rear more young in total this way than by monogamous nesting. A Canadian study has shown that some females are deceived into forming a harem by an initially promising supply of food by the male, which is not kept up. In Orkney the frequent dominance of one female in the harem was recorded, to whom most food was delivered. Elsewhere, monogamous nesting can be fairly closely spaced over prime open heather moorland. Semi-colonial nesting is possible because the area defended around the nest is not large on the ground but takes on the shape of a bubble, with intruders being edged out by the resident male from below. In less productive habitats nests can be separated by 2 km (1¼ miles) or more.

Montagu's harriers can nest in groups of perhaps ten or more nests fairly regularly spaced over favoured expanses of rank vegetation. In one study in Poland, the mean nearest-neighbour distance between nests was 130 metres (142 yards), but nests were found just 20 metres (22 yards) apart. In Britain, because of the small population, the semi-colonial nesting recorded has consisted of only small groups of up to about five nests. Polygyny is known to occur in this species.

Polygyny in the marsh harrier is usually restricted to one male serving two females. At sites where there is competition to breed, the oldest males are the polygynous ones. Also, distribution of breeding birds takes on a clumped aspect because nests are generally restricted to the reed-beds in a locality, but the tendency towards colonial nesting is not as strong in the marsh harrier as in the other British harriers. This may be because of the larger food intake and therefore greater competition for resources in this larger species.

REGULATION OF BROOD SIZE TO FOOD SUPPLY

The breeding success of harriers is largely dependent on the abundance of prey and fine weather, which allow the adults to hunt effectively. The eggs are generally laid at intervals of one to three days and incubation is begun early in the clutch. This results in asynchronous hatching and a wide age range amongst the brood. At first, the young are fed small pieces of prey by the female, which can result in a reasonably fair distribution, although younger chicks may be hidden and starve if the larger ones are always hungry enough to reach up. When they are more mobile, the young grab food from the female and defend it, mantling it and striking out when others try to snatch a piece. Repeated and prolonged attacks on the smaller young are sometimes fatal. At some sites the young make tunnels through surrounding vegetation along which they can retreat from the nest a short distance. This behaviour could have evolved to avoid predators or to avoid the nest becoming too fouled, but young have been observed finding the tunnels useful to block rival young in with their wings whilst they feed on newly delivered prey. When there is an abundance of food, competition will be less because the larger young are not hungry when further food is brought in for the others.

HEN HARRIER

A bird of moorland of moderate height in the breeding season, the hen harrier generally nests amongst thick heather or rushes encouraged by dampness of the ground, which can be thick with sphagnum moss in places. Occasionally grasses, bracken or other rank vegetation dominate at nest sites, which are generally on rolling terrain or on hillsides, on open ground or in young conifer plantations. Nest sites are generally traditional and, although sites may not be used every year, a nest often tends to be built in the same general area if birds are present.

19. *Hen harrier food pass. (Left) The female rises from the nest upon hearing the food call of the male; (centre) he drops the prey which she catches in mid air; (right) he usually flies away and she descends to the ground to prepare the food.*

The hen harrier begins to return to its breeding grounds from about February but generally should be in place by early April. Mid April is a prime time to watch courtship display. At intervals, on fine days, a pair will soar up together, the male gently circling one way and the female perhaps the other and below him. Over moorland which has emerged from a night's frost into bright sunshine, this is often a beautiful prelude to the 'sky-dance' display. In full display, the male takes on the properties of a yoyo in the sky, diving vertically a great distance and rising again almost vertically back to the same height. Occasionally the female joins suit. Sometimes there will be many consecutive dives, with the bird loosely waving its wings and making a distinctive chatter. Less full-bodied display is of the 'switchback' variety, when the bird undulates at a much lower height across the site. The most distinctive call made by the female at this time is an importuning wail. At other times, and in between hunting forays away from the place, the pair will be associating over the site and investigating thoroughly low over the area, the female often inconspicuous apart from her white rump and the light-coloured male conspicuous against dark heather or dark green conifers.

19

The nest is built by the female with pieces of uprooted heather and the stems of other plants. It is lined with grasses. Generally four or five eggs are laid, in late April or May. Hatched at 29-31 days, young are brooded continuously by the female until they are ten to fifteen days old. After this they become active enough to move into neighbouring vegetation. They fledge at 32-42 days.

MARSH HARRIER

Nearly all marsh harrier nest sites in England are in common reed (*Phragmites australis*) or similar 'reed-bed' type vegetation, such as great fen sedge (*Cladium mariscus*). In recent years, however, as a response to saturation of reed-bed sites in at least one area of Norfolk, several nests have been built in arable crops such as winter cereals. It used to be thought that large reed-beds were essential for this species to breed. However, in recent years the success of pairs in very small reed-beds in favoured areas has shown this not to be the case. The overall environment of the area seems to be the important factor, with flat coastal plains containing some wetland being populated first and inland sites less readily. One important factor affecting distribution

may be the inability of the species to hunt in the rain. Eastern England has a very low summer rainfall.

On favoured breeding grounds where a number of birds arrive in April there is much high circling by males. Sometimes a male high in the sky will suddenly flap with stiff accentuated wing-beats or dive, often in stages, towards the ground, incorporating aerobatics of variable complexity and screaming out loud. Where pairs are isolated, there may not be much display at all and the business of nesting can proceed with great speed. Often males arrive at a site and even without a female present begin building a platform, only to give up soon and go elsewhere.

The nest is built by both female and male, a fairly bulky platform of reed or similar vegetation less than a metre across. The male will also build platforms or 'cock's nests' of his own, on to which he will often fly with prey or to roost.

Clutches of as few as two eggs and as many as eight have been found, but the norm is four or five, laid in April or May. Hatching at 31-8 days, the young begin to grow feathers through their white down at about fifteen days from hatching. The male, which may have been loitering or hunting largely over nearby marsh during

20. *Female Montagu's harrier and young.*

incubation, can suddenly switch to hunting away over surrounding open farmland, where a heavier biomass of food can be obtained more easily. He brings in prey about once an hour to a full-sized brood, and the female begins to hunt, adding more and more to the supply, from when the young are about ten days old. They fly at 35-40 days but are still dependent on an adult for up to about 25 days more. Often just one adult remains with them, but experience is divided as to whether it is generally the female or the male.

MONTAGU'S HARRIER

The later breeding season of this species, which arrives at breeding sites late in April or in May, suits the use of autumn-sown 'winter' cereal crops for nest sites, which by then are well grown. Before the development of these early-growing crops, Montagu's harrier bred in young conifer plantations, on heathland and marshes where rank ground vegetation was available. Recently it has been rare to find a nest in these more natural habitats. The open prairie-like landscape of much of arable Britain may allow some increase in the population of Montagu's harrier, but there are problems in finding them in these large areas not frequented by birdwatchers and where nests are likely to be destroyed by farming operations. Spraying of a nest may be tolerable before the eggs hatch, but it is especially dangerous to young. Also, harvesting may in many cases occur before the young fledge. Arrangements can be made to leave that section of crop until later. Alternatively, young have been successfully moved during harvesting, either to a nearby false nest, or to be put back later in the same place protected by straw bales. Elsewhere in western Europe, large organised campaigns have to be conducted to protect nests from combine harvesters. Especially prominent in this work is the French organisation Fonds d'Intervention pour les Rapaces.

The preliminaries to nesting of this graceful species are wonderful to observe. The male often arrives first to establish a territory and the female a few days later. For his sky-dance display the male circles up high above the site.

21. *Male hen harrier climbing and falling in sky-dance display above his mate.*

Following him with binoculars is difficult in shimmering heat or if it is at all misty. At some point he will bend back his wings into a fast glide and then plunge in dives of varying intricacy, pulling up in stages, twisting as he falls and finishing with a deft swoop into the very place chosen or diving on his mate. The female may spend many hours over a few days flying and gliding low over the chosen ground, inspecting it all over. In between, each bird flies off to hunt away from the site.

The nest is usually built by the female, being a mound of whatever vegetation is available, about half a metre (1 foot 8 inches) across. The most frequent clutch is four eggs, but as few as two and as many as twelve have been recorded, laid in the second half of May or June. As might be expected with a smaller species, the incubation period is shorter, at 28-9 days. The young begin to grow feathers through their white down about fifteen days after hatching and tunnel into surrounding vegetation when they become mobile. They fledge at 35-40 days.

Communal roosting

Outside the breeding season a harrier's existence is based around the communal roost. Speculation is rife as to the function of communal roosting in birds, with warmth, mutual warning of the approach of predators and exchange of information on good feeding areas being the most discussed. Although many types of birds roost communally at regular sites, harrier roosts are different to most because they are situated on the ground, amongst rank vegetation. Since the same sites are generally used nightly, this seems to be a dangerous way of spending the night and bound to attract predators to stalk the harriers. However, harriers' good hearing is doubtless an important protection, and the strongly communal nature of these roosts may facilitate some sort of mutual warning mechanism important for survival. The harriers roost individually in gaps in the vegetation and on flattened patches or tussocks, often within a few metres of each other, but sometimes much further apart. They gain no warmth from each other, but the choice of terrain and vegetation at sites seems to be governed, at least partly, by considerations of shelter. Although individuals

have been found killed by foxes (*Vulpes vulpes*) where they have been successfully stalked during the night, this is rare, and at roosting time harriers may react to such a predator *en masse* by diving on it and calling in alarm.

In autumn in East Anglia communal roosts of marsh harriers form in crops such as barley, wheat, beans and sugar beet. As many as thirty birds have been observed coming together to roost in the same field in areas where several pairs had been breeding a few weeks earlier. Marsh harrier roosts can also be found on marshes at that time. A few Montagu's harriers sometimes frequent the same areas and roost nearby. Numbers tend to build up later in August and into September, with a fairly sudden exodus in mid September as nearly all marsh harriers set off on migration for Africa. A very few remain to winter and are encountered at several wetland winter roost sites of the hen harrier.

Hen harriers roost in a variety of open habitats. About half of the sites found in the British Isles are on fresh or salt marsh in reed, sedge, rush, grass or other rank vegetation. Other sites are on dry rough grassland, in heather on lowland heath or heather moor, and occasionally in dunes, young conifer plantations and crops. The great majority of roosts in the east of England are no more than 15 metres (50 feet) above sea level, but roosts in other

22. *Young Montagu's harriers. This species often nests in crops and, as at this nest, the vigorous surrounding growth may have to be cut back to prevent the nest being smothered.*

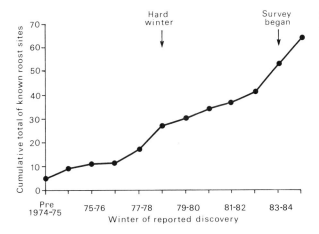

23. *Pattern of the enormous increase in reported discoveries of regular communal hen harrier winter roosts in England since the mid 1970s. Data from the Hen Harrier Winter Roost Survey, a BTO Trust-aided enquiry.*

regions have been found at altitudes of up to 427 metres (1400 feet). Roosts of up to thirty or more birds have been recorded, but they usually comprise just a few birds and even single birds persist in using the same sites.

Approaching the site from about three-quarters of an hour before sunset, the birds will often fly about, criss-crossing each other's flight paths over the site. A fresh wind is often used for soaring about in the vicinity. Commonly, a pre-roost gathering of birds will form on short grass or bare ground nearby, flying in to roost nearer to dusk. Before they begin to settle finally, there may be a moment when all or most of the birds are in the air together. At other times, especially in rain or when there is little wind to assist flight, birds may arrive and roost immediately with no more than one or two in sight at any one time. The larger females sometimes oust males from roosting places, which then often fly to and fro, hesitating over possible places and perhaps landing a few times before they finally settle for the night. By about half

an hour after sunset all birds will have finally settled.

Chattering calls are occasionally heard at hen harrier roosts, usually as the birds dive on something unseen in the long vegetation. Otherwise, the roost spectacle seems strangely silent, but a quiet high-pitched squeal made by harriers displacing others from where they have settled or in other confrontation is frequent, but rarely heard by observers.

Harriers leave their roost from about half an hour before sunrise, occasionally settling to preen before flying out of the area. They may leave singly in all directions, or in twos or threes in a particular favoured direction. They travel quite a distance from the roost site during the day; the maximum published distance is 16 kilometres (10 miles) for the hen harrier. There is some evidence that hen harriers maintain individual hunting ranges in winter. Towards sunset, harriers can be seen flying directly to a communal roost, using the same roost for an unpredictable period of days, weeks or months.

ACKNOWLEDGEMENTS

Illustrations are acknowledged as follows: S. Redpath, cover; J. White, 1, 2, 13; D. Darton and the author, 3, 4; D. Hollands, 5; S. Danko, 6, 7, 9, 14, 17, 20, 22; B. Pearson, 8, 19; P. Steyn, 10; W. S. Clark, 11; D. MacCaskill, 12, 18; G. Hewson and the author, 15; J.-Ch. Tombal, 16; D. Watson, 21.

Further reading

Balfour, E., and Cadbury, C. J. 'Polygyny, Spacing and Sex Ratio among Hen Harriers *Circus cyaneus* in Orkney, Scotland', *Ornis Scandinavica*, 10 (1979), 133-41.

Clarke, R. 'The Diet of Hen Harriers Roosting in Wicken Fen', *Cambridgeshire Bird Report* (1988).

Clarke, R., and Watson, D. 'The Hen Harrier *Circus cyaneus* Winter Roost Survey in Britain and Ireland', *Bird Study*, 37 (1990), 84-100.

Cramp, S. and Simmons, K. E. L. (editors). *The Birds of the Western Palearctic*, 2. Oxford University Press, 1980.

Lack, P. *The Atlas of Wintering Birds in Britain and Ireland*. T. and A. D. Poyser, 1986.

Marquiss, M. 'Habitat and Diet of Male and Female Hen Harriers in Scotland in Winter', *British Birds*, 73 (1980), 555-60.

Picozzi, N. 'Dispersion, Breeding and Prey of the Hen Harrier *Circus cyaneus* in Glen Dye, Kincardineshire', *Ibis*, 120 (1978), 498-508.

Picozzi, N. 'Food, Growth, Survival and Sex Ratio of Nestling Hen Harriers *Circus c. cyaneus* in Orkney', *Ornis Scandinavica*, 11 (1980), 1-11.

Picozzi, N., and Cuthbert, M. F. 'Observations and Food of Hen Harriers at a Winter Roost in Orkney', *Scottish Birds*, 12, 3 (autumn 1982), 73-80.

Sharrock, J. T. R. *The Atlas of Breeding Birds in Britain and Ireland*. T. and A. D. Poyser, 1976.

Sills, N. 'Marsh Harriers at Titchwell Marsh Reserve (1980-1983)', *Norfolk Bird and Mammal Report* (1983 and 1984), 342-8 and 84-95.

Underhill-Day, J. C. 'Population and Breeding Biology of Marsh Harriers in Britain since 1900', *Journal of Applied Ecology*, 21 (1984), 773-87.

Underhill-Day, J. C. 'The Food of Breeding Marsh Harriers *Circus aeruginosus* in East Anglia', *Bird Study*, 32, 3 (November 1985), 199-206.

Watson, D. *The Hen Harrier*. T. and A. D. Poyser, 1977.

Organisations

British Trust for Ornithology (BTO), Beech Grove, Tring, Hertfordshire HP23 5NR. Researches Britain's birds — breeding patterns, the movement of migrants, the growth and decline of populations and habitats, and the effects of changing environments. Data are based on survey work by members, for use by the government and conservation bodies to protect Britain's birds.

Hawk and Owl Trust, c/o Zoological Society of London, Regent's Park, London NW1 4RY. Working for the conservation of all birds of prey.

International Council for Bird Preservation (ICBP), 32 Cambridge Road, Girton, Cambridge CB3 7BR. Devoted to the conservation of birds and their habitats, on an international scale.

Irish Wildbird Conservancy (IWC), Southview, Church Road, Greystones, County Wicklow, Ireland. Similar aims to the BTO, but in Ireland.

Royal Society for the Protection of Birds (RSPB), The Lodge, Sandy, Bedfordshire SG19 2DL. Takes action for wild birds and the environment.